Favorite BIBLE STORIES

Activities for Grades 1&2

Author .... *Carolyn Passig Jensen*

Cover Design .... *Court Patton*

Illustrator... *Fran Kizer*

Rainbow Publishers®
Copyright 2003 • Fifteenth Printing
Rainbow Publishers • P.O. Box 261129 • San Diego, CA 92196
www.rainbowpublishers.com

#RB36243
ISBN 0-937282-16-2
church and ministry/ministry resources/children's ministry

CONTENTS

OLD TESTAMENT ACTIVITIES

NEW TESTAMENT ACTIVITIES

BIBLE-TEACHING ACTIVITIES

Introduction

One of the best ways to teach children biblical truths and Christian attitudes is through Bible stories. In fact, the hundreds of interesting and exciting stories which fill the Bible make spiritual truths come alive and help children learn how to live the Christian life through the examples of real people and their victories and struggles.

This book provides 52 exciting, Bible-learning activities built around 26 favorite Bible stories and biblical principles from both the Old and New Testaments. As your first and second-graders do these activities, they will learn not only the facts and events of the Bible stories, but also what the stories teach and how to apply it to their own lives.

There are two different exciting Bible-learning activities, on side-by-side pages, for each Bible story. The teacher may choose to use either or both of the activities in teaching the Bible story. You may make multiple copies of all activity sheets for the children.

You'll find a great variety of activities suitable for a variety of teaching situations and all designed for the abilities of children in the first and second grades — coloring, cutting, pasting and folding activities, puppets, mazes, simple counting and reading activities, connect-the-dots, hidden pictures, find and circle activities and many more exciting projects.

All the activities are designed to supplement and compliment the teaching of favorite Bible stories and to be used in the classroom under the direction of a teacher or leader. These activities are prepared with the assumption the children have already been told the Bible story. The purpose of these activities is to reinforce the teaching of the Bible story and to help the children apply the biblical lesson to their own lives.

Each activity sheet features short introductory paragraphs which refer to the Bible story and give step-by-step instructions for the activity. The paragraphs are designed to be read to the children or, if possible, for the children to read themselves. The top of the page also lists the Bible story and scriptural reference. (The King James Version of the Bible is used.)

A special "For the Teacher" section at the bottom of the pages, gives valuable teaching tips, hints for using the activity, discussion ideas, or further instructions just for the teacher. The teacher will want to cover this section prior to duplicating copies so these teaching ideas do not appear on the children's papers. The pages of the book are perforated so they may be easily removed for duplication.

All of the activities in this book have been designed to be simple and easy to do, with minimal preparation for the teacher. All necessary patterns, figures and cut-outs are included, full size, to ensure successful projects every time.

Most activities require only ordinary school supplies or household items. Care should always be taken to ensure the safety of the children when using scissors, staples, pencils and all other items which can potentially cause harm.

Children are sure to look forward to your class and the opportunity to work on these fun and exciting activities. And the wide variety of different learning projects are sure to keep the children asking for more of these favorite Bible story activities!

Favorite BIBLE STORIES

Activities for Grades 1 & 2

Old Testament

God created the heavens and the earth. He made the night and the day. Then God made the oceans, mountains, and all the living things on the earth.

On the circle, color the DAY yellow and color the NIGHT black. Then draw a line from the yellow side of the circle to things that usually happen in the daytime. Draw a line from the black side of the circle to things that usually happen at night.

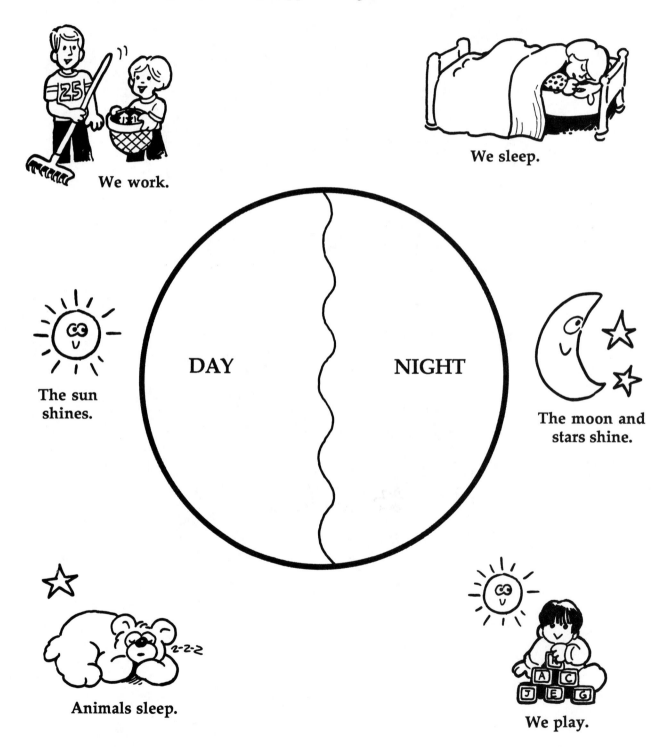

We work.

We sleep.

The sun shines.

DAY   NIGHT

The moon and stars shine.

Animals sleep.

We play.

For the Teacher: Help children read the words on the circle and the captions under the pictures. Talk about nighttime and daytime activities. Emphasize the greatness of God's creation to the children.

Things God Made

God created our world and our universe. He made the heavens and the earth. He made the moon and the stars. He made oceans, rivers, mountains and valleys. God also created all the plants and animals and birds. He created you, too.

Color the pictures of the things God made. Leave uncolored the things which people have made.

Stop and say a prayer of thankfulness to God for the wonderful things He made.

Tree

Telephone

Giraffe

Cat

Dog

Flowers

Car

House

 For the Teacher: Help the children understand the difference between things God made in the beginning and things which people make using the things God made in the beginning. Example: God made trees. People cut down the trees and use the wood to build houses and furniture.

9

Adam and Eve
Genesis 1:26 — 2:25

Adam and Eve were the first man and woman God created. God also made Adam and Eve a beautiful garden where they could live. The garden had everything Adam and Eve needed.

God told Adam and Eve not to eat the fruit on one special tree, but a wicked snake came and told Eve to eat the fruit anyhow. Eve ate the fruit and gave some to Adam. God punished Adam and Eve for disobeying Him by sending them away from their garden home.

Find and color five things from Adam and Eve's garden home which are hidden in the picture.

 For the Teacher: Help the children understand Adam and Eve's disobedience and that as a result we are all sinners. Emphasize to the children that Jesus came to earth to die and come alive again so our sins can be forgiven when we ask Him. Offer the opportunity for the children to pray with you for forgiveness. (The five hidden items are Adam, Eve, tree, snake, fruit.)

What Animal is It?

After God created Adam and the rest of the world, God told Adam to name all the animals.

Draw a line from each animal picture to the description of the animal. If you know how to write the animal's name, write it on the line after the description.

Think about other names Adam could have given the animals. What would you name them?

A yellow animal with brown spots and a very long neck.

_____

An animal that seems to have long arms instead of front legs. A funny animal that makes us laugh.

_____

A large, furry animal. May be black or brown or white. Sometimes we have furry toys like this animal.

_____

A small animal that many people have as a pet. Comes in many colors. Says, "Meow."

_____

This animal is called the "king of the beasts." It is strong and fierce. It is a light brown color.

_____

This animal is a well-liked pet. It has been called "man's best friend." It comes in many colors, and it barks.

_____

 For the Teacher: Lead the children in thanking God for the animals (and other creations) He made. To help the children remember Adam named the animals God created, the children could draw an imaginary animal on another sheet of paper and give it a name.

Noah and the Ark
Genesis 6:8 — 8:22

God's Promise Mobile

The people on the earth were very sinful. God told Noah to build a big boat and take his family and every kind of animal into the ark, because God was going to destroy the sinful people in a big flood. Noah trusted and obeyed God. The flood came and all living things outside the ark died.

Inside the ark, God took care of Noah, his family and the animals. After the flood, God put a beautiful rainbow in the sky and promised He would never again kill all living things by a flood.

You can make a pretty mobile to help you remember to trust in God and obey Him. Color and cut out the mobile shapes and punch holes at the top. Your teacher will give you a plastic clothes hanger and yarn to tie the figures to the hanger. Learn the memory verse.

Trust in the Lord, and do good. *Psalm 37:3*

For the Teacher: Discuss what it means to trust in the Lord and do good and help the children learn the verse together. Put a small piece of tape over each piece of yarn tied on the hanger.

Food for the Animals

God told Noah to take two or more of every animal into the ark to protect them from the flood. Noah took care of the animals and fed them the food they needed.

Draw a line from the animals on the left to the food they eat on the right. Can you read the names of the animals and their foods?

Then say thank You to God for the good food He gives you to eat every day.

Cow

Milk

Cat

Grass

Bird

Peanut

Elephant

Worm

 For the Teacher: Talk about how Noah took care of the animals. Discuss foods needed by other animals not pictured. Say, "God protected all the animals in the ark during the flood. He wanted the animals to be able to live on the earth again after the flood." Relate God's care for the animals to God's care for us.

A Wife for Isaac
Genesis 24

Follow the Path to Find Rebekah

Abraham knew his son Isaac needed a wife. He sent his servant to find a girl to marry Isaac. Follow the path to see what happened. Then color the pictures.

Abraham asks his servant to find a wife for Isaac (1). The servant gets on his camel and rides to another country (2). The servant asks God to have the girl God wants to marry Isaac offer to water the servant's camel (3). Rebekah comes to the well and waters the camel (4). Rebekah and the servant return to their country (5) and Rebekah marries Isaac.

 For the Teacher: Use this story to teach the children we should tell God our problems and He will help us. Discuss problems the children may have which they can tell God about. Give time for silent prayer for the children to tell God their needs. Close by thanking God for hearing and answering our prayers.

14

A Wife for Isaac
Genesis 24

Isaac was very happy when his father's servant brought Rebekah home to be his wife. He knew God had given him a very special wife.

Color and cut out the picture of Isaac and the figure of Rebekah. Tape a small strip of paper to the back of Rebekah. Slip a string through the paper strip and tape the two ends of the string on the picture at the dots. Move Rebekah to meet Isaac.

 For the Teacher: It is not too early to begin to teach the children that God has a perfect plan for their lives. Say, "God had a special plan for Isaac and Rebekah to be married. God has a special plan for your life. It is important to always obey God so we are always doing what God has planned for us."

Baby Moses

Exodus 2:1-10

Color by Number

A wicked king wanted to kill all the baby boys born to God's people. To protect Baby Moses, his family hid him in a basket boat on the river. Moses' sister, Miriam, hid in the weeds near the river to be sure Moses was safe. God helped a kind princess find Moses' basket bed and she made sure he was not killed. Moses became her adopted son. God is a great God who loves and cares for His people. He loves and cares for you.

Follow the directions to color the picture of Baby Moses, Miriam and the kind princess.

1 — Green
2 — Blue
3 — Brown
4 — Yellow

 For the Teacher: Discuss with the children how God took care of Baby Moses. Help them to understand that God is taking care of them just as He took care of Baby Moses.

A Basket for Baby Moses

To keep Baby Moses safe from a wicked king who wanted to kill the baby boys, Baby Moses' mother made a very special basket boat for him. She covered a basket with some material like glue to keep the water out. Then she put Baby Moses in the basket and put the basket in the river. Miriam hid in the weeds to be sure Moses was safe. A kind princess found Moses and kept him safe. God took care of Baby Moses.

Color and cut out the pictures of Baby Moses and the basket. Glue Baby Moses onto the basket. Remember God took care of Baby Moses and God is taking care of you.

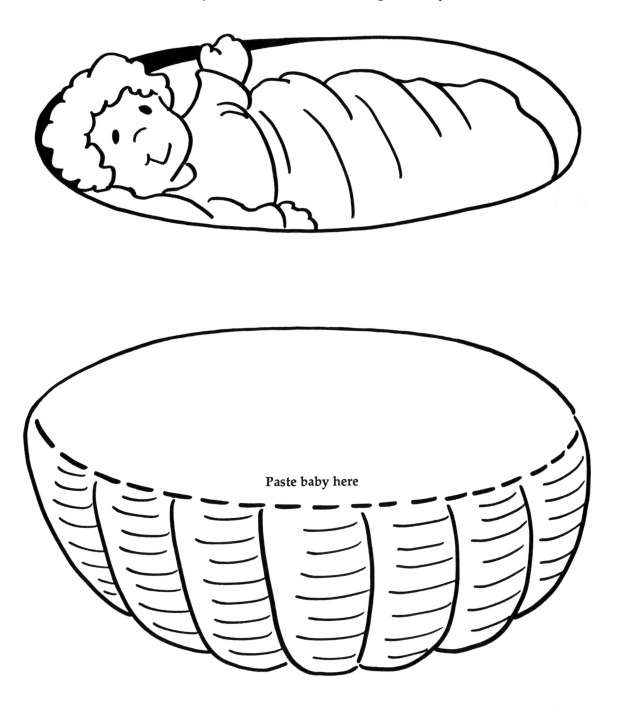

Paste baby here

 For the Teacher: Tell the children of God's special plan for Moses to grow up and help deliver his people from another wicked king. Then say, "God has a special plan for your life too. It is important that you obey God so you can follow God's plan for your life."

17

God's People Leave Egypt
Exodus 7 — 14

Moses and Pharaoh
Finger Puppets

God's people had lived in Egypt for a long time, but the wicked king Pharaoh did not like them. He made them work very, very hard and was very cruel to them. God wanted His people to leave Egypt and go to live in a new country. God chose Moses to tell Pharaoh to let God's people leave.

Moses went to see Pharaoh, but Pharaoh would not let God's people go. God made a stick turn into a snake to show Pharaoh His power, but Pharaoh still said, "No!" God sent many plagues on Egypt until finally Pharaoh said God's people could go.

Color and cut out the finger puppets of Moses and Pharaoh. Your teacher will help you cut out the holes and fold the puppets so they fit on your fingers. Use the puppets to tell the story of Moses and Pharaoh.

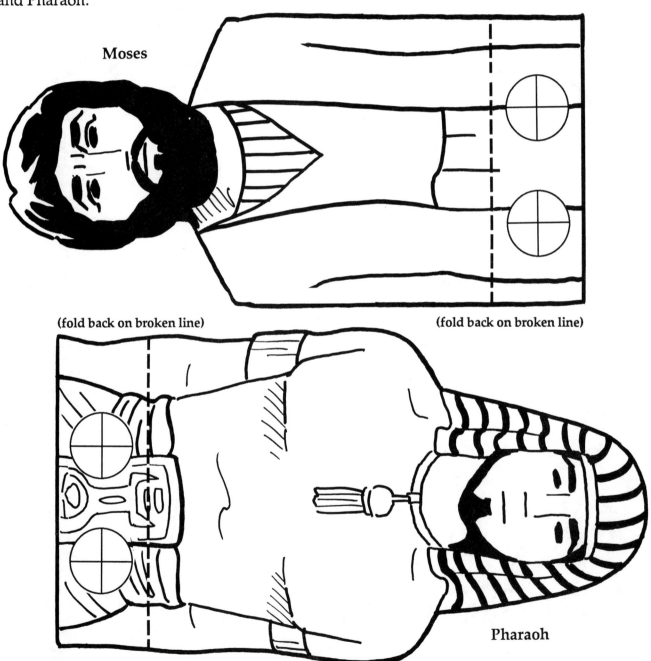

Moses

(fold back on broken line)   (fold back on broken line)

Pharaoh

 For the Teacher: Duplicate one set of puppets for each child. Glue the puppet to construction paper or poster board prior to class. An adult should use a craft knife to cut out the holes for the children's fingers.

18

What did Pharaoh Say?

The wicked king Pharaoh in Egypt did not like God's people. He made them work very, very hard and was very cruel to them.

God wanted His people to leave Egypt and go to live in the country God promised them. God told Moses to go and tell Pharaoh to let God's people leave Egypt. Pharaoh said, "No!"

God did many miracles to show Pharaoh His power, but Pharaoh still said, "No!"

Trace the broken lines in each picture. Fill in the blanks with the correct words. What did Pharaoh finally say?

God sent _____ . "Pharaoh said, "_____!"

God sent _____ . "Pharaoh said, "_____!"

God sent _____ . "Pharaoh said, "_____!"

 For the Teacher: Help the children understand God's power in bringing the plagues. Then say, "Pharaoh should have done what God wanted right away. Finally, God made the oldest child of every family die. Then Pharaoh said God's people could leave Egypt. We should always obey God right away too."

Picture Puzzle

God's people needed some rules so they would know how to obey God. God gave them ten special rules we call the Ten Commandments. Your teacher will read them with you. Moses went up on a mountain and God wrote the Ten Commandments on two stone tablets. God wants His people to know and follow these special rules in everything they do.

Color and cut out the picture on the heavy black lines. Cover both sides of the picture with clear adhesive-backed plastic and then cut the picture apart on the broken lines. You can put your puzzle together to help you remember the Ten Commandments God gave us to follow.

 For the Teacher: Read and discuss each commandment with the children. Say, "God's rules are good rules. If we follow them we will be happy and God will bless us."

Obeying God's Commandments

God wants us to follow the Ten Commandments He gave His people in the Bible. Your teacher will read the Ten Commandments with you.

Read each of the sentences below. Color the picture in front of each statement if the child is obeying one of God's commandments. Cross out the picture if the child is disobeying God.

 Jerry put a toy truck in his pocket and ran out of the toy store.

 Terry broke his mother's new vase, but he told his mother his little sister did it.

 Sarah did not dust the living room when her mother said to do it.

 Danielle said, "I'll tell the truth. Danny didn't take the money."

 Cindee went to Sunday school and church this week.

 Ryan waited until Sunday night to do his homework.

 All the children in Jason's class use bad words. Jason doesn't use bad words.

 Andrew said, "I wish I had that shiny new model car Peter has."

 Melissa said, "I sure wish we had the Masons' house. It is so big and pretty."

 Sharon is making a doll house at home. At school, her teacher had some special wooden sticks for making crafts. Sharon took some home when her teacher wasn't looking.

 For the Teacher: Use the situations above to lead the children into practical discussions of how to obey the Ten Commandments in situations they face. Help the children decide which commandment is or is not being obeyed in each situation.

David Serves God
I Samuel 17; II Samuel 2

Reasons to Praise God

David loved God and tried to obey Him. David took care of his father's sheep. Once a lion attacked the sheep, but God helped David kill it. Another time, David killed a bear who tried to hurt the sheep. When a giant named Goliath made fun of God's people, everyone was afraid, but David knew God would help him kill Goliath too.

David had many reasons to be thankful to God. He wrote many beautiful songs praising God and telling God thank You for His care.

Use colored chalk to color the pictures which show why David praised God. Then your teacher will help you to make up your own praise song to God.

 For the Teacher: Colored chalk soaked for a few minutes in one part sugar and three parts water will color nearly as brightly as crayons. After coloring, sing a praise song the children know and then guide the class in writing words for their own song of praise which can be sung to a familiar tune.

22

King David's Crown

When David grew up, He became the king of the country of Israel, the nation of God's people. David tried to be a good king and obey God. David praised God and wrote many beautiful songs of thankfulness to God. Some of these songs are printed in our Bible in the Book of Psalms.

You can make a crown to wear to act out the stories of King David. Cut a crown out of yellow or gold construction paper using the pattern below. Decorate your crown with materials your teacher gives you. Your teacher will help you staple a narrow construction paper strip to each side of the crown at the large dot and help you make the crown fit your head.

Your teacher will help you sing some songs of praise to God while you wear your crown.

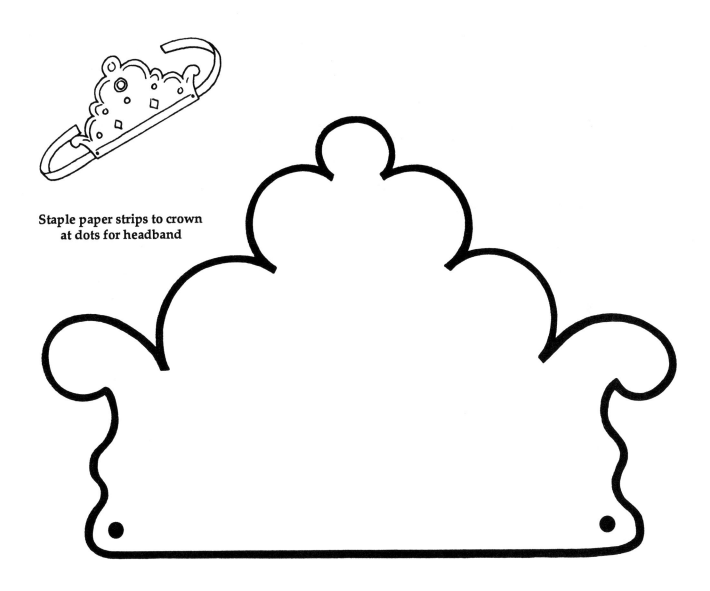

**Staple paper strips to crown
at dots for headband**

 For the Teacher: Provide sequins, small squares of aluminum foil or shiny gift wrap or other materials with which to decorate the crowns. Staple the ends of the headbands together to fit each child's head. Sing praise songs the children know while they wear their crowns.

God's Word is Found
II Kings 22 & 23

Color by Number

The scroll with God's Word written in it had been lost for a long time. One day someone found it and brought it to King Josiah. Josiah read God's Word to the people. "From now on we will obey what God's Word says," he told them. "We will love God and keep His laws. We will do what God wants us to do." God was happy King Josiah wanted the people to hear God's Word and obey it.

The Bible is God's Word for us. God wants us to read and obey the Bible too.

Follow the instructions to color the picture of King Josiah reading God's Word to the people.

1 — Yellow
2 — Blue
3 — Red
4 — Green

 For the Teacher: You may wish to make a scroll by rolling a sheet of paper between two pencils to use in telling this story. Read selected Scriptures to the children from the scroll. You might also hide the scroll in your classroom and let the children find it. The one who finds it may read from it to the class.

24

God's Word is Found
II Kings 22 & 23

King Josiah was happy when God's Word was found and He and the people could learn what God wanted them to do. We should be happy because we have the Bible, God's Word, all the time to tell us how to obey God.

Read the story about another treasure that was found. Why did Jenny think the Bible is a treasure Book?

A Real Treasure

 decided to look for treasure. She looked under

the , but she only found an old . She looked

in the but only found .

Then looked inside an old trunk. She found a

 and a and a shiny . "I found a treasure!"

said Jenny.

Then found an old . She read the title. The

 was a . "I found a real Treasure!" said Jenny.

"The is a Treasure Book from God!"

For the Teacher: Discuss why the Bible is a Treasure Book. What should we do with the Bible each day? Ask the children to name things found in the Bible which make it a Treasure to us.

The king made a huge idol and told the people they must kneel down and worship it. Three men would not worship the idol because God says we are not to worship anyone but Him.

Follow the path to see what happened to the three brave men, named Shadrach, Meshach and Abednego (1): The other people bowed down to worship the idol, but Shadrach, Meschach and Abednego did not (2). They told the king they would not worship the idol (3). The king had the men thrown into a fiery furnace, but Jesus appeared in the flames with the men (4). The king had the men brought out of the furnace. They were alright! God saved them from the fire (5)!

This story teaches us we should always obey God no matter what other people are doing.

 For the Teacher: Talk about (or act out) situations in which the children may be asked to do things which are not pleasing to God. Help the children realize what is wrong about each activity and guide the children in knowing how to say no.

What Would You Do?

Shadrach, Meshach and Abednego were very brave. They did not worship the idol the king made even when they knew the king would throw them into a fiery furnace. God protected them from the fire and many people believed in God.

Sometimes people want us to do things that are disobedient to God too. Look at the pictures of children who are disobeying God. Would you do the same thing if someone asked you? Draw a happy face beside the pictures of actions you would not do and draw a sad face beside the actions you would do. If we ask Him, God will help us to do right even if other people laugh at us.

Be mean to animals.

Steal money.

Tease someone.

Be angry at someone.

Fight.

Disobey parents.

 For the Teacher: Talk about each situation pictured and help the children identify why it is wrong. Then let them make their own decision whether or not they would do the activity and draw the appropriate face in the circle. You may wish to teach the children Deuteronomy 6:18a as a memory verse.

Daniel in the Lions' Den
Daniel 6:4 – 22

Story Sequence

Daniel was a good man. He knew God would take care of him, even when the king put him into a den of hungry lions because he prayed to God every day.

Color the pictures that tell the story of Daniel. Number them in the order they happened. Then draw the king's face. Was the king happy or sad God protected Daniel from the lions?

We should always obey God even when other people try to get us to disobey God.

 For the Teacher: After the children have put the pictures in order, ask for a volunteer to tell the story of Daniel, as review, using the pictures as a guide.

Lion Puppet

God did not let the hungry lions hurt Daniel. God took care of Daniel because he obeyed God.

Color the lion puppet and cut it out. Your teacher will show you how to glue your lion to a paper sack to make a puppet.

Use the puppet to act out the story of Daniel. One child may pretend to be Daniel while the rest of the class wears their puppets. Pretend to be hungry lions and roar loudly. When Daniel comes into the room, shut the lions' mouths and be very quiet.

For the Teacher: Show the children how to glue their puppets to lunch-size paper sacks. Demonstrate how to operate the puppet and help the children act out the story of Daniel.

Activities for Grades 1 & 2

New Testament

Make a Christmas Mural

Jesus was born in a stable, where cows and sheep usually sleep. Mary, Jesus' mother, laid Jesus in a manger, the place where the animals usually ate their food. God put a beautiful star in the sky over Bethlehem. God wanted the whole world to know Jesus, His Son was born.

You can make a pretty Christmas mural to help you celebrate Jesus' birthday. Fold a sheet of construction paper in half. Place the broken lines on the pattern along the fold of the construction paper. Cut out the pattern along the heavy black lines, being sure to cut through the pattern and the construction paper. Unfold the construction paper and glue your manger and star on a contrasting sheet of construction paper. Below the manger, write "Jesus is born."

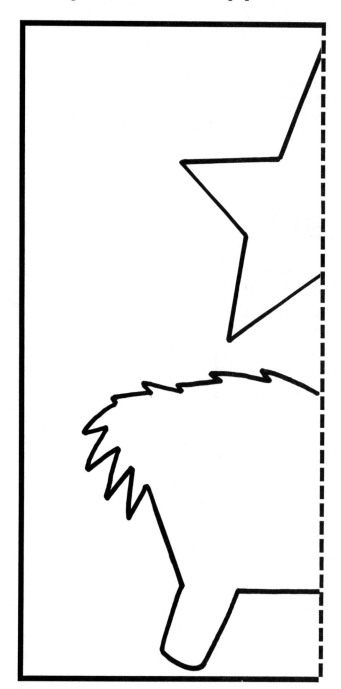

Jesus is born.

 For the Teacher: Younger children may need some assistance with holding their pattern and cutting at the same time.

Shepherd Child Puppet

When Jesus was born, God sent an angel to tell some shepherds that Jesus, God's Son had been born. The shepherds hurried to the stable to worship Baby Jesus.

Color and cut out the shepherd child puppet. Your teacher will show you how to glue the puppet to a paper sack. Pretend you were one of the shepherds who saw the angel and went to worship Jesus. Tell about what you saw when you visited Baby Jesus, God's Son, in the stable where He was born.

 For the Teacher: Show the children how to glue their puppet to a lunch-size paper sack and how to operate the puppet. Allow the children to take turns using their imaginations to tell what they might have seen when they visited the stable where Jesus was born.

An Angel Tells of Jesus' Birth
Luke 2:10-14

Nativity Stick Puppets

When Jesus was born, an angel told some shepherds who were caring for their sheep, that Jesus was born. The shepherds hurried to the stable where Jesus was born and worshipped Him.

Color and cut out the figures below. Your teacher will show you how to glue them onto ice cream sticks or tongue depressors. Use your puppets to act out the story of Jesus' birth.

Shepherds

Mary, Joseph, and Baby Jesus

Angel

 For the Teacher: Before class, glue the figures for each child on a sheet of construction paper or poster board. Help the children glue on the ice cream sticks or tongue depressors. Let the children take turns holding the puppets while the story is told. An inverted shoe box, with slits cut in the bottom, can be used to hold the puppets upright when not in use.

Stand-up Angel

The angel God sent to the shepherds told them that Jesus, God's Son, was born in Bethlehem. Then the angel was joined by other angels who sang "Glory to God in the Highest" and praised God.

Color the angel and cut it out. Roll back the angel's robe, overlapping A over B and fasten with a staple. Take your angel home to remind you to praise Jesus like the angels who sang praises when Baby Jesus was born.

 For the Teacher: The angel will stand better if glued to a sheet of construction paper before coloring and cutting. Help the children bend the skirt into a circular shape before stapling.

35

The Lord's Prayer

Matthew 6:9-13

Learning to Pray
Picture Puzzle

Jesus taught His disciples a special prayer. We call it the Lord's Prayer. It teaches us how to live close to Jesus and do what He wants us to do. Praying the Lord's Prayer helps us to know what to pray and how to ask God for our needs.

Count the disciples in the picture. How many are there?

Color the picture and cut it out along the heavy black line. Cover both sides of the picture with clear adhesive-backed plastic. Then cut the picture apart along the broken lines. Can you put the puzzle back together so you can see all 12 of Jesus' friends as they learn to pray?

 For the Teacher: Begin teaching the children the Lord's Prayer, phrase by phrase, over several class sessions. Be sure to explain each phrase as you go. Perhaps you will want to keep the puzzles in your class for the children to work each week as a visual reminder of the Lord's Prayer they are learning.

Stand-up Card

The Lord's Prayer
Matthew 6:9 – 13

The Lord's Prayer is a special prayer Jesus taught His disciples. Jesus wants His followers to pray the Lord's Prayer because it helps us live close to Jesus and do what He wants us to do. The Lord's Prayer also helps us to know what to say when we pray and how to ask God for our needs.

You can make a special stand-up card to help you learn and remember the Lord's Prayer at home. Fold a half-sheet of construction paper in half. Color the pictures and cut them out. Glue the picture of Jesus to the front of the construction paper folder and glue the Lord's Prayer on the inside. Read or say the Lord's Prayer with the rest of the class. At home, you can use your stand-up card to help you read or say the Lord's Prayer every day.

The Lord's Prayer
Matthew 6:9 – 13 (KJV)

Our Father which art in heaven, Hallowed be thy name.

Thy kingdom come, They will be done in earth as it is in heaven.

Give us this day our daily bread.

And forgive us our debts, as we forgive our debtors.

And lead us not into temptation, but deliver us from evil: For Thine is the kingdom, and the power, and the glory, for ever. Amen.

For the Teacher: Prepare half-sheets of construction paper before class. Show the children how to fold their sheet in half to make a folder. Encourage them to do their best work in coloring the picture of Jesus. When the folders are complete, lead the class in reading or saying the entire Lord's Prayer. Continue memorization of the Lord's Prayer. (See page 36.)

Find the Hidden Pictures

Jesus loves children. When He lived on earth, He was very happy when children came to see Him. He held the children in His arms and He blessed them.

Now that Jesus is in heaven, He still loves children. He loves you and He can be with you all the time. He wants to be your Friend if you will ask Him.

Look at the picture. Jesus *likes* trees, flowers, grass and other things, but He *loves* children. There are 10 hidden flowers in the picture. Can you find them? How many children are there who Jesus loves?

 For the Teacher: Talk about ways we know Jesus loves us. Include Jesus' willingness to die for our sins as one way we know He loves us. Give the opportunity for children to ask Jesus to be their Friend and Savior.

My Best Friend Bookmark

When Jesus was on earth, He liked to have children for friends. Jesus wants to be your Friend now. He is the Best Friend you can ever have. He will be with you all the time. He will help you and comfort you. He will help you to know what is the right thing to do.

You can ask Jesus to be your Best Friend right now. Say, "Dear Jesus,. I want You to be my Friend and Savior. Please forgive me for the wrong things I have done. In Jesus' Name. Amen."

The bookmark below will help you remember Jesus is your Best Friend. Color the picture and cut out the bookmark. Cover both sides with clear, adhesive-backed plastic. Trim the plastic neatly around the edges. Tie a piece of yarn through a hole at the top of the bookmark.

For the Teacher: Use this activity to present the plan of salvation and give the opportunity for the children to accept Jesus as their Savior and Friend. The children may draw themselves beside Jesus, if desired.

Jesus Heals a Paralyzed Man
Luke 5:18-26

Help the Friends Find Jesus

Jesus was preaching in a house. Some men carried their friend who was paralyzed because they wanted Jesus to heal him. There were so many people listening to Jesus, the men could not get in.

The men made a hole in the roof and lowered their friend to where Jesus was preaching. Jesus healed the man and he walked home!

Help the friends of the sick man find the way to Jesus so their friend can be healed. Then help the man find his way home after Jesus healed him.

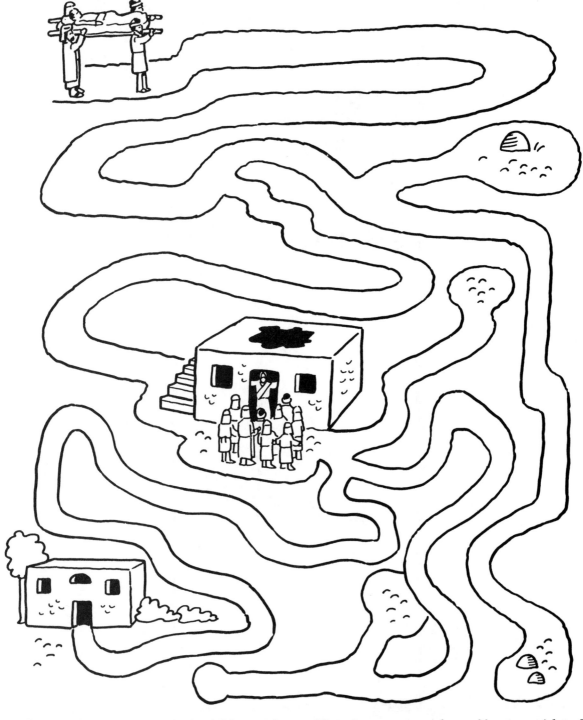

 For the Teacher: Help the children understand Jesus' power over sickness. You may wish to discuss some of Jesus' other miracles. Begin to teach the children that Jesus is God, Jesus and Christ — the same Person.

Shoe Box House

Jesus Heals a Paralyzed Man
Luke 5:18-26

The paralyzed man's friends wanted him to be healed so much they made a hole in the roof and lowered their friend down into the house to Jesus. Jesus healed the man and he walked home!

Color and cut out the picture of the man. Glue the bed to a piece of poster board. Punch a hole in each corner of the bed at the large dot and tie a piece of string or yarn through the hole. Fold the picture of the man along the broken line and glue to the bed.

Make a house by cutting a hole about 7 by 3-1/2 inches in the bottom of a shoe box. Decorate the outside of the shoe box with markers and cut out windows and doors. Turn the shoe box house upside down and lower the man on his bed through the hole in the roof.

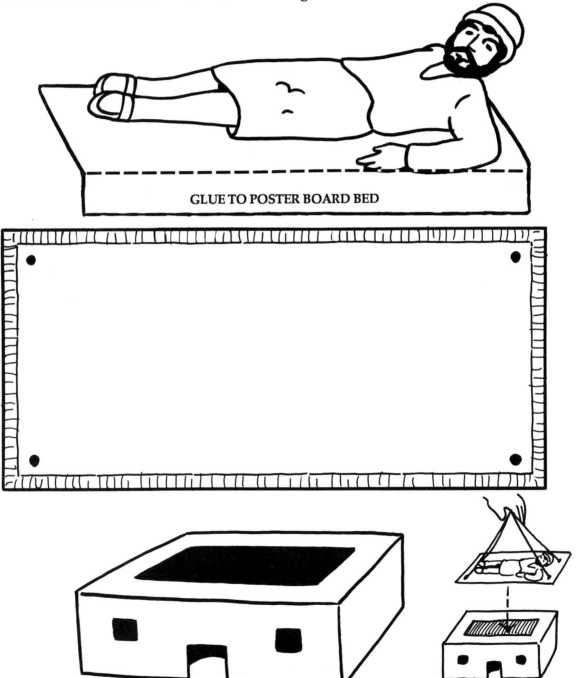

GLUE TO POSTER BOARD BED

 For the Teacher: Assist the children in gluing the man to the bed and in tieing the yarn or string through the holes. Tie the four strings together above the bed to make it easier to lower the bed into the house.

The Lost Sheep
Luke 15:4-7; John 10:27

Count the Sheep

Jesus told a story about a Good Shepherd who cared for His sheep. When one sheep got lost, the Good Shepherd looked and looked for the sheep. When He found the sheep, the Good Shepherd carried the sheep home and took care of it. The Good Shepherd was very happy He found the sheep.

Jesus loves us and takes care of us like the Good Shepherd took care of His lost sheep.

Count the sheep inside the fence. The shepherd should have 10 sheep. How many are missing? Where is the lost sheep? Follow the directions to color the picture by number.

1 — White
2 — Brown
3 — Blue

For the Teacher: Talk with the children about how a shepherd cares for his sheep. Emphasize the importance of the sheep following and obeying their shepherd. Help the children understand that Jesus loves and cares for them and they should obey Him.

Stand-up Lamb

The Lost Sheep
Luke 15:4-7; John 10:27

Jesus told a story about a Good Shepherd who looked and looked for a sheep which was lost. The Good Shepherd was very happy when He found the lost sheep.

Jesus loves us and takes care of us like the Good Shepherd took care of His lost sheep.

You can make a stand-up lamb to help you remember Jesus loves you and cares for you. Color the picture of the lamb and glue it to a piece of construction paper. When the glue is dry, cut it out.

Use the heart pattern to cut a red heart out of construction paper. Write on the heart, "Jesus Loves Me." Glue the heart onto the lamb.

Your teacher will help make your lamb stand by putting its feet in a slit cut in half a paper tube.

 For the Teacher: If class time is short, glue the lambs to construction paper before class so the glue is dry and children can color and cut out without waiting for drying time. Also before class, cut cardboard tubes (such as found in bathroom tissue) in half lengthwise, and cut a slit about 3-1/2 inches long in the top of the tube. You will insert the lamb's feet into the slit so the lamb stands upright as shown.

The Run-away Boy
Luke 15:11-32

Draw How He Looked

Jesus told the story about a boy who ran away from home. When he had no more money, he got a job feeding pigs. He was so hungry, he would have liked to eat the same food the pigs ate.

The boy was sorry for what he had done and he decided to go home. His father forgave him and had a big party to welcome him back home.

Just like the boy's father, Jesus will forgive us when we are sorry we have done wrong things.

The boy probably had nice clothes when he left home. On the picture, draw how the boy looked when he was hungry and feeding the pigs. You can draw some of the pigs too.

How do you think the boy looked after his father forgave him?

 For the Teacher: Help the children to begin to understand the consequences of sin. Emphasize Jesus' willingness to forgive and offer an opportunity for the children to ask Jesus to forgive them.

Find the Way Home

Jesus told an important story about a man who had two sons. Follow the path and color the pictures to learn the story:

The father gave one son some money. The other son stayed home and worked hard (1). The first son left home and wasted all his money (2). He was so hungry, he wanted to eat the food the pigs ate (3). At last, he decided to go back home (4). When he came home, his father was very happy and gave a big party to welcome him.

Jesus will forgive us when we are sorry we have done wrong things, like the boy's father forgave him.

 For the Teacher: Although first and second graders will not understand much symbolism, they can understand that Jesus will forgive them, like the father forgave his run-away son. Help any children who wish to do so to pray to ask Jesus to forgive them and become their Savior.

Zacchaeus was a very short man. He wanted to see Jesus, but there were so many people, he couldn't see Jesus at all. So he climbed up in a tree.

When Jesus came by, he told Zacchaeus to come down and they had lunch at Zacchaeus' house. Jesus forgave Zacchaeus for the wrong things he had done.

Follow the maze to help Zacchaeus find the best branch in the tree where he can see Jesus.

For the Teacher: Talk with the children about Zacchaeus' determination to see Jesus and Jesus' forgiveness. Help the children realize that Jesus forgives sins. All they have to do is ask Jesus to be their Savior.

Finger Puppets

Zacchaeus
Luke 19:1-10

Zacchaeus really wanted to see Jesus, so he climbed up in a tree. Jesus told Zacchaeus to come down and they went to his house for lunch. Zacchaeus told Jesus he was sorry for the wrong things he had done. Jesus forgave him.

When we ask Him, Jesus will forgive us for the wrong things we do too.

Color the finger puppets of Jesus and Zacchaeus and cut them out. Your teacher will help you put your puppets together so you can use them to act out the story of Zacchaeus.

Jesus

Zacchaeus

 For the Teacher: Assist the children in taping the ends of the tabs together and putting the puppets on their fingers. The children may take turns playing Jesus and Zacchaeus.

Jesus Heals a Sick Boy
John 4:46-54

A Happy Boy

A very important man came to see Jesus. "Please, Jesus," the man said, "Come quickly! My boy is very sick. Please come and make him well again."

Jesus gently said, "You can go home again. Your son lives!" The man went home and found his boy was well just as Jesus said!

Color the dotted sections to find the happy boy Jesus made well.

 For the Teacher: This story can help the children begin to understand that Jesus' power is not limited by time or place. Emphasize that Jesus healed the little boy without even seeing him.

When You are Sick

Jesus Heals a Sick Boy
John 4:46-54

When Jesus was on earth, He made many people well. One person Jesus made well was a little boy whose father came to Jesus. Now that Jesus is in heaven, He still makes people well.

Sometimes, Jesus uses doctors and medicines to help us get well. Sometimes, Jesus heals people who the doctors couldn't help at all.

Color the pictures of things you should do when you are sick to help you get well. Cross out the things you should not do when you are sick.

Spread germs around other people.

Stay in bed and rest.

Take the medicine my parents give me.

Go outside and play.

Go to the doctor.

Pray and trust God.

Eat candy and potato chips.

 For the Teacher: Help the children understand Jesus is caring for them even when they are sick and they do not need to be afraid. You may wish to teach Hebrews 13:6 (NKJV) as a memory verse.

Jesus Rides Into Jerusalem
Matthew 21:1-16

Story Strip

Jesus was going to Jerusalem. "Go to the next village. You'll find a donkey and a colt. Bring them to me," Jesus told His disciples (1). Jesus got on the donkey (2) and rode toward Jerusalem. The people were very happy to see Jesus. Some of the people waved green palm branches in the air. The people worshipped Jesus and sang praises to Him. The children sang to Jesus too (3).

Color and cut out the story strip. Your teacher will make two slits in an index card. Slide your story strip through the slits so one picture shows at a time. You can use your story strip to tell the story of Jesus and to help you remember to praise Jesus too.

 For the Teacher: An adult should use a craft knife to cut two slits about 2-1/4 inches long and 2-inches apart in an index card. Show the children how to slide the strip through the slits so only one picture shows. Let the children take turns using their story strip to retell the story.

50

Color, Cut and Paste

One day Jesus rode a donkey into Jerusalem. The people were very happy to see Him. Some of the people waved green palm branches in the air. Some of the people took off their coats and laid them on the road. The people worshipped Jesus and sang praises.

Color and cut out the pictures of Jesus, the donkey and the people. Glue the donkey on a sheet of construction paper and glue Jesus on its back. Glue some fabric scraps on the road for the donkey to walk on. Glue the people on the construction paper and glue green leaves in their hands.

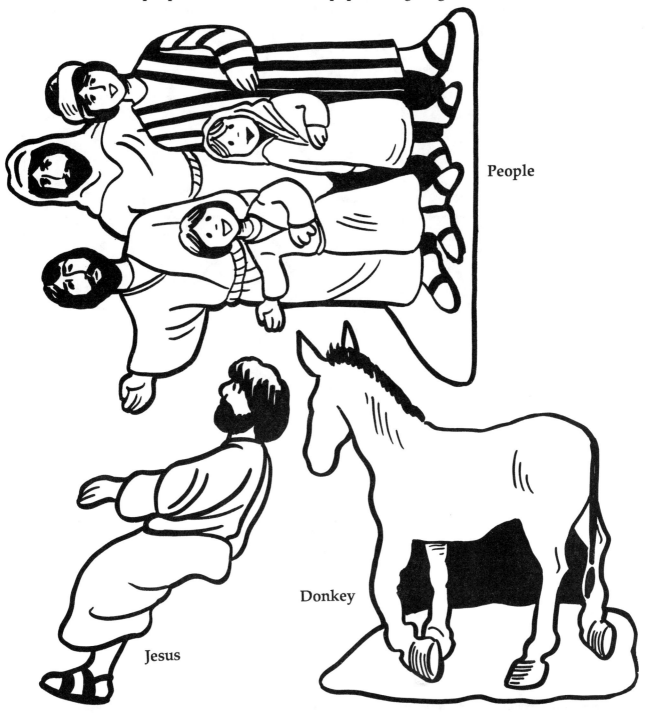

People

Donkey

Jesus

 For the Teacher: Real green leaves, artificial leaves or leaves cut out of construction paper may be used on the picture. Talk about how we can worship Jesus. Lead the children in singing praise choruses they know.

Jesus Dies and Comes Alive Again
Matthew 27 & 28

Colorful Cross

Jesus loves us and cares for us so much He died so we can be forgiven for the wrong things we do. Jesus took the punishment we deserved for our sins. When we ask Him, Jesus will forgive us for our sins.

To see where Jesus died, color the dotted sections red. Then color the rest of the sections other pretty colors. Then glue your picture to a sheet of construction paper.

 For the Teacher: Simply and clearly present the plan of salvation and offer the chance for the children to ask Jesus to forgive them and be their Savior. Help the children glue their picture to a sheet of construction paper.

Easter Week Circle

Jesus Dies and Comes Alive Again
Matthew 27 & 28

At Easter, we celebrate Jesus' death, His burial and His resurrection. Resurrection means Jesus came alive again. Jesus died and came alive so we can be forgiven for our sins.

Glue your circle on a sheet of construction paper or poster board. Color the pictures and cut out the circle. Your teacher will help you cut a large, triangular wedge out of a dessert-sized paper plate and fasten it over your circle with a paper fastener. You can turn the paper plate to see what happened at the first Easter.

Jesus died
on the cross

I sing for joy!

Jesus was
buried

Jesus rose from
the dead

 For the Teacher: If class time is short, glue the circles to construction paper or poster board before class, so children do not have to wait for glue to dry. Assist the children in putting their circle and paper plate together. Tape down the prongs of the paper fastener to prevent scratching. After using the circle to review the Easter story, lead the children in singing songs of praise for Jesus' resurrection.

Paul Tells About Jesus
Acts 13 — 28

People Who Heard About Jesus

Paul traveled all around his world telling people about Jesus. Sometimes people were happy to hear about Jesus. Sometimes what Paul said about Jesus made them mad. Paul did not let anything stop him from telling people that Jesus would forgive their sins.

Paul was one of the first missionaries. Missionaries are people who go far away to tell about Jesus.

Look at the picture of Paul preaching to the people. How should people look when they hear about Jesus? Draw faces on the people showing how they should look when they hear the Good News about Jesus. Then color the picture.

 For the Teacher: Begin to help your students understand that they can tell people about Jesus like Paul did. Prepare them for the fact that some people will be happy to hear and some will not. Help them think of people they can tell about Jesus this week.

54

Places to Tell About Jesus

Paul Tells About Jesus
Acts 13 — 28

Paul told many people all over his world about Jesus. You can tell people in your neighborhood about Jesus too.

Follow the trail to help Katie find her way from her house to her school, her church, the playground, a friend's house and the grocery store. You can tell people about Jesus at all these places.

Who can you tell about Jesus this week?

For the Teacher: As the children follow the trail to each location, discuss who they can tell about Jesus at that place. Help the children plan what they can tell people about Jesus. You may wish to act out some situations so the children can practice telling someone about Jesus.

Favorite
BIBLE STORIES
Activities for Grades 1 & 2

Bible-teaching
Activities

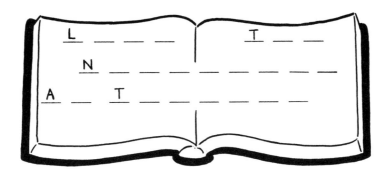

L _ _ _ _ _ T _ _

N _ _ _ _ _ _ _ _

A _ _ T _ _ _ _ _ _ _

The Bible is God's Book
Psalm 119:16; John 5:39

The Bible is God's Book. It is like a special letter from God to us. The Bible tells us wonderful stories of God's power and miracles. The Bible gives us solutions to our problems.

God wants us to learn and remember what the Bible says. You can make a bookmark to put in your Bible to help you remember to read and learn from the Bible each day.

Cut two bookmarks out of construction paper, using the pattern below. Your teacher will cut two slits in one of the bookmarks. Slip a piece of ribbon 8-1/2 inches long through the slits. Glue the second bookmark to the back to hold the ribbon in place. Decorate your bookmark with stickers or cut-outs and write on the bookmark something you want to remember from the Bible.

 For the Teacher: Talk about some of the things the Bible teaches us (Jesus loves us. Jesus died for our sins. God is love, etc.) and let the children choose what they want to write on their marker. Help the children find a favorite verse in their Bible, mark it and place their bookmark in that page.

Read a Story

The Bible is God's Book

Psalm 119:16; John 5:39

God gave us the Bible to help us know how to obey Him. The Bible gives us the solutions to our problems. Read the story to learn how the Bible helped one boy named Kenny.

How the Bible Helped Kenny

Kenny did not like the lady who lived next door. Her name was Mrs. Gable. Kenny thought Mrs. Gable was really mean.

Mrs. Gable didn't want any children to take even one little step inside her yard. Every day, Mrs. Gable sat on her porch in her big rocking chair and watched the children come home from school. If any of the children stepped on her grass, she yelled, "Get off my lawn this minute!"

One day Kenny and his friends were playing ball in Kenny's backyard. Ryan, Kenny's friend, hit the ball and it flew over the fence into Mrs. Gable's yard. "Keep your toys in your own yard," Mrs. Gable growled at Kenny and Ryan.

Kenny never talked to Mrs. Gable when he saw her on the porch. He didn't even smile at her. He tried to not even look at her. Kenny thought Mrs. Gable was really mean.

Then one day Kenny learned a special verse from the Bible. He learned how God wanted him to act toward Mrs. Gable.

The next day on his way home from school, Kenny saw Mrs. Gable sitting on her porch, in her big rocking chair, as usual. But today, instead of not talking to Mrs. Gable, instead of not smiling at Mrs. Gable, and instead of not looking at Mrs. Gable, Kenny waved and smiled. "Hi, Mrs. Gable," he said.

Look up Matthew 22:39 in your Bible. Choose the five words that you think helped Kenny to do right. Write the five words in the blanks below.

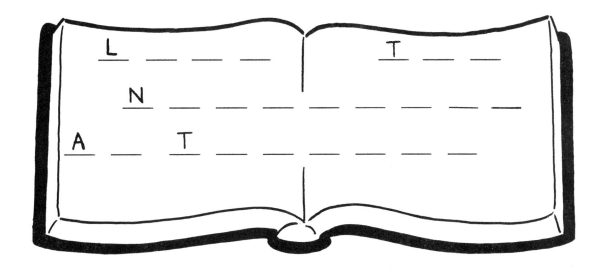

For the Teacher: Help the children to read the story together. Discuss what it means to love our neighbors as ourselves. Let the children talk about other ways they can show love to people around them.

Prayer
Psalm 4:3

Prayer is talking to God. We can talk to God any time. We can talk to God from any where, and we can talk to God about any thing.

You can tell God how you feel even when you can't tell any one else. When you are wanting to obey Him, God will always hear you when you pray.

Write the number of the sentence which tells when you can pray in the space beside the picture which shows when you can pray. What other times can you talk to God?

Then draw a picture of yourself talking to God.

1. I can talk to God at night when I am in bed.

2. I can talk to God when I am playing and having fun.

3. I can talk to God when it is time to eat.

4. I can talk to God when I am afraid.

Draw yourself talking to God:

 For the Teacher: In addition to the situations shown, talk about other times the children can pray. Talk about things the children can tell God. Then guide each child to talk to God in a simple sentence prayer.

Connect the Dots

Prayer
Psalm 4:3

God wants us to talk to Him any time. Sometimes it is hard to pray, because there are many people around or it is noisy. God will hear your prayer anyway.

When you pray, you can tell God thank You for the good things He does for you. One good time to say thank You to God is before we eat our food.

Follow the dots to see what the boy is doing before he eats his lunch. Sometimes people might laugh at you for praying, but Jesus is with you to help you do what He wants you to do.

 For the Teacher: Discuss situations in which others might laugh at the children for obeying the Lord. Help the children understand that the Lord will help them to obey Him no matter what.

Obeying Parents
Ephesians 6:1

God wants you to obey and love your parents. Sometimes you might not want to obey your parents, but Jesus will help you to do what is right.

One way you can show your parents you want to obey them is to help them at home and keep your room clean and neat.

Michael and Jason need to help their parents by making their yard look neat. Color all the things Michael and Jason can clean up or put away. Did you find all 14 things?

What things can you do to obey your parents and keep your house neat?

 For the Teacher: Help the children to think of other situations in which they might not want to obey, but Jesus will help them. Discuss why obedience to parents shows Jesus we want to obey Him too.

Helper Certificate

When you obey your parents, you are obeying God. The Bible tells children to obey their parents.

Sometimes it is hard to obey, but Jesus will help you do what is right.

You can show your parents you want to obey them by giving them this Helper Certificate. Write in your name, the name of the person you will obey by helping, and what job you will do for them. Color the seal your favorite color and cut out the certificate. Give the certificate to the person you want to help.

Helper Certificate

I, _____
(Your Name)

will help

_____
(Name of person you will help)

by doing

_____
(job)

_____

(Signed) _____

For the Teacher: Brainstorm with the children jobs they can do to show obedience to their parents. You might suggest they use their helper certificate to show their parents they will do some job they have been unwilling to do before. Help the younger children fill in the blanks, if needed.